ONE BIG RAIN

Poems for Rainy Days

COMPILED BY
Rita Gray

Illustrated BY
Ryan O'Rourke

ini Charlesbridge

TABLE OF CONTENTS

INTRODUCTION

Autumn is stunning. Trees grow colors, the sky blazes blue, and fields bulge ready for harvest. It's a time of change. The falling rain and wailing winds gradually pluck the trees bare. We move inside to the warmth of our homes, happy for the inside weather.

Winter helps rain put on a magic show. Presto! Cold rain transforms into sleet, snow, and ice. When winter rain grows silent, we know that lacy snow is falling in its place. Winter is a time of harsh beauty; even the stars seem colder.

The first rains of spring melt away the last snow of winter making way for new life. Flowers bloom, shoots sprout, leaves unfold. Frogs, snails, and birds come out with the wet, and so do we. We stomp in puddles and squish in mud. We watch the sky smile a rainbow.

Summer means hot, humid days when the air feels as wet as the inside of a honeydew. We wish it would rain—big, fat drops by the barrelful—a crashing, bashing, flashing rain. When the sky finally lets loose, what a show! Summer rain is sweet relief.

A gentle rain can shower, sprinkle, drizzle, or mist. Powerful rains beat down in storms and downpours, fall in streams and sheets, or race, rush, and gush in torrents. Rain can play a pinging beat as it falls willy-nilly from the sky: pitter-patter, plip-plop, drip-drop, plink-plink. And puddles are perfect to splish-splosh. Poets have captured the language and rhythm of the rain, creating images that stay with us throughout the year.

As you read about rain, in various poetic forms,
Ripple in it, float in it, boat in it.
Go on, get wet.

—Rita Gray

ABOUT HAIKU TRANSLATIONS

Haiku usually show something in one season or another. Haiku began in Japan, but haiku form varies from one language to another, because no two languages have quite the same rhythms or sound patterns. When we translate a haiku from one language to another, we have to find the best rhythm for it in the new language.

To write a haiku in English in a form like the Japanese, give your poem three short lines, with the middle line the longest. Use words that show things people can see, hear, taste, touch, or smell—or some combination. If you see the way a thing looks, hear the way it sounds, and can put words together so that other people see and hear the same in their minds, you can write haiku. Enjoy!

—Adapted from *Wind in the Long Grass: A Collection of Haiku,* by poet and translator William J. Higginson.

Haiku

—Kyôtai

the falling leaves
fall in layers . . . the rain
beats on the rain

Black Cat

—Rita Gray

Black cat
at a white
window-pane
watches a rose
run red
in the rain.

The Mist and All

—Dixie Willson

I like the fall,
The mist and all.
I like the night owl's
Lonely call—
And wailing sound
Of wind around.

I like the gray
November day,
And bare, dead boughs
That coldly sway
Against my pane.
I like the rain.

I like to sit
And laugh at it—
And tend
My cozy fire a bit.
I like the fall—
The mist and all.

November Rain

—Maud E. Uschold

This autumn rainfall
 Is no shower
That freshens grass
 And brings the flower.

This rain is long
 And cold and gray,
Yet sleeping roots
 Are fed this way.

Trees and bushes,
 Nearly bare
Of leaves, now chains
 Of raindrops wear

Along each twig.
 Some clear beads fall.
A tree could never
 Hold them all.

Haiku

—Kyoshi

on the broad hat
stolen from a scarecrow
how hard the rain

WiNTER

Haiku

—*Shisei-jo*

under an umbrella
pushed back by the force
of this winter rain

Blizzard
winds

while a
sparrow

scratches
the snow

for summer.

—*Richard Lewis*

Weather Report

—*Lilian Moore*

Pinging rain
stinging sleet
tonight.

Frost at dawn,
bright
sun in the
morning.

Ice-bearing trees,
a glass
orchard,
blinking
sunwinking.

A noonwind will
pass,
harvesting the brittle crop,
crashing
clinking.

Haiku

—Sora

stars on the pond—
again, a pitter-patter
of winter rain

To the Thawing Wind

—Robert Frost

Come with rain, O loud Southwester!
Bring the singer, bring the nester;
Give the buried flower a dream;
Make the settled snow-bank steam;
Find the brown beneath the white;
But whate'er you do to-night,
Bathe my window, make it flow,
Melt it as the ices go;
Melt the glass and leave the sticks
Like a hermit's crucifix;
Burst into my narrow stall;
Swing the picture on the wall;
Run the rattling pages o'er;
Scatter poems on the floor;
Turn the poet out of door.

SPRING

Haiku

—Rogetsu

tree-frogs
calling . . . in the young leaves
a passing shower

Little Snail

—Hilda Conkling

I saw a little snail
Come down the garden walk.
He wagged his head this way . . . that way . . .
Like a clown in a circus.
He looked from side to side
As though he were from a different country.
I have always said he carries his house on his back . . .
To-day in the rain
I saw that it was his umbrella!

Rain

(Translated from the Norwegian by Sarah J. Hails)
—Sigbjørn Obstfelder

One is one, and two is two—
we sing in huddles,
we hop in puddles.
Plip, plop,
we drip on roof top,
trip, trop,
the rain will not stop.
Rain, rain, rain, rain,
bucketing rain,
chucketing rain,
rain, rain, rain, rain,
wonderfully raw,
wet to the core!
One is one, and two is two—
we sing in huddles,
we hop in puddles.
Plip, plop,
we drip on roof top,
trip, trop,
the rain will not stop.

The Sower

(Translated from the Spanish by Dudley Fitts)
—R. Olivares Figueroa

On a white field,
black little seeds . . .
> *Let it rain! rain!*

'Sower, what do you sow?'
How the furrow sings!
> *Let it rain! rain!*

'I sow rainbows,
dawns and trumpets!'
> *Let it rain! rain!*

Haiku

—Issa

a bush warbler . . .
muddy feet wiped
on the plum blossoms

SUMMER

Haiku

—*Sodô*

a lone watermelon
knows nothing of the storm
this morning after

Summer Rain

—Eve Merriam

A shower, a sprinkle,
A tangle, a tinkle,
Greensilver runs the rain.

Like salt on your nose,
Like stars on your toes,
Tingles the tangy rain.

A tickle, a trickle
A million-dot freckle
Speckles the spotted rain.

Like a cinnamon
Geranium
Smells the rainingest rain.

Release

—*A. R. Ammons*

After a long
muggy
hanging
day
the raindrops
started so
sparse
the bumblebee flew
between
them home.

Haiku

—Yosa Buson

hit by
a raindrop—
the snail closes up

Summer Grass

—Carl Sandburg

Summer grass aches and whispers.

It wants something; it calls and sings; it pours
out wishes to the overhead stars.

The rain hears; the rain answers; the rain is slow coming;
the rain wets the face of the grass.

Acknowledgments

AUTUMN

"Black Cat" by Rita Gray. Copyright © 2005 by Rita Gray. "The Mist and All" by Dixie Willson, reprinted by permission of Dana Briggs. "November Rain" by Maud E. Uschold (public domain).

WINTER

"Untitled" by Richard Lewis, reprinted by permission of the author. Copyright © 2007 by Richard Lewis. "Weather Report" by Lilian Moore, from Lilian Moore, *Something New Begins* (New York: Atheneum, 1982); reprinted by permission of Marian Reiner. Copyright © 1967, 1969, 1972, 1975, 1980, 1982 by Lilian Moore. "To the Thawing Wind" by Robert Frost (public domain), from Robert Frost, *A Boy's Will* (London, David Nutt, 1913).

SPRING

"Little Snail" by Hilda Conkling (public domain), from Hilda Conkling, *Poems by a Little Girl,* (New York: F. A. Stokes Co., 1920). "Rain" by Sigbjørn Obstfelder, English translation by Sarah J. Hails, reprinted by permission of Hails House Translations. English translation copyright © 2008 by Sarah J. Hails. "The Sower" by R. Olivares Figueroa, translated by Dudley Fitts, from Dudley Fitts (ed.), *Anthology of Contemporary Latin-American Poetry* (Norfolk, CT: New Directions, 1947); reprinted by permission of New Directions Publishing Corp. Copyright © 1947 by New Directions Publishing Corp.

To William J. Higginson (Bill), 1938–2008,
with gratitude—R. G.

For my wonderful wife, Trishy—R. O.

Compilation copyright © 2010 by Rita Gray
Illustrations copyright © 2010 by Ryan O'Rourke
All rights reserved, including the right of reproduction in whole or in part in
any form. Charlesbridge and colophon are registered trademarks of
Charlesbridge Publishing, Inc.

Published by Charlesbridge
85 Main Street
Watertown, MA 02472
(617) 926-0329
www.charlesbridge.com

Library of Congress Cataloging-in-Publication Data
One big rain : poems for rainy days / compiled by Rita Gray ;
illustrated by Ryan O'Rourke.
    p. cm.
Includes bibliographical references and index.
ISBN 978-1-57091-716-5 (reinforced for library use)
1. Rain and rainfall—Juvenile poetry. 2. Seasons—Juvenile poetry. 3.
Haiku—Translations into English. 4. Children's poetry. 5. Children's
poetry, American. I. Gray, Rita. II. O'Rourke, Ryan, ill.
PN6110.R35O54 2010
811.008'036—dc22   2009026748

Printed in China
(hc) 10 9 8 7 6 5 4 3 2 1

Illustrations done in oil on paper
Display type and text type set in Humble Bee and Dante
Color separations by Chroma Graphics, Singapore
Manufactured by Regent Publishing Services, Hong Kong
Printed February 2010 in ShenZhen, Guangdong, China
Production supervision by Brian G. Walker
Designed by Susan Mallory Sherman